Sixty Fingers, Sixty Toes

See How the Dilley Sextuplets Grow

BECKI AND KEITH DILLEY

PHOTOGRAPHS BY E. ANTHONY VALAINIS

Walker and Company

New York

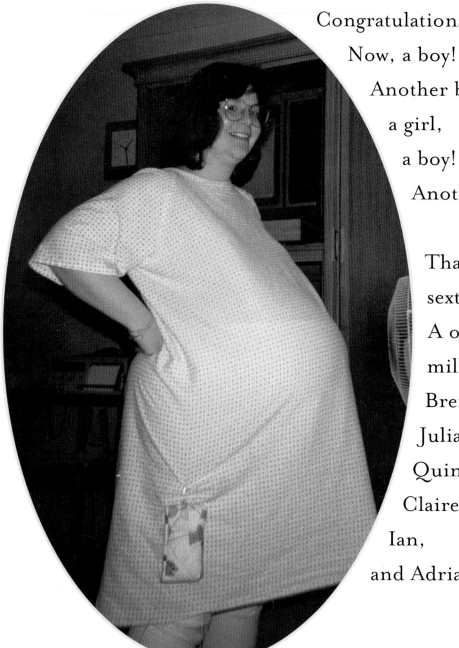

Congratulations, it's a girl!
Now, a boy!
Another boy,
a girl,
a boy!
Another boy!

That makes six—
sextuplets.
A one in a hundred
million chance.
Brenna,
Julian,
Quinn,
Claire,
Ian,
and Adrian.

Six weeks later, the babies can
be brought home from the hospital.

Life is like musical chairs.
Six babies sleep in three cribs.
They don't leave much time
for the grown-ups to rest.

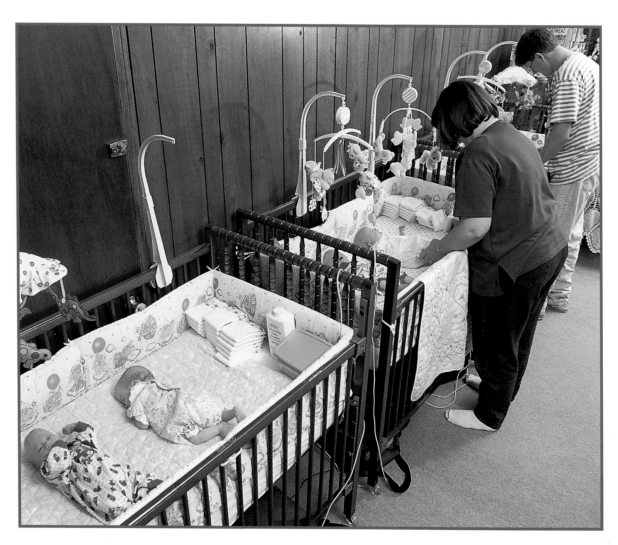

A diaper change at 11 P.M.

Another diaper change at 1 A.M.

Feed Brenna, feed Julian, feed Quinn.

By 4 A.M., Dad's hardly slept.
Now it's Mom's turn to watch the babies.

In the morning,
Mom goes to work as a nurse and—
Surprise!—
Mr. Mom stays home.

With forty-two bottles,
forty diaper changes,
and three loads of laundry,
the day flies by.
Dad doesn't feel much like a
celebrity,
but guess what?

The sextuplets are *instant* celebrities.
They star in a TV commercial
about a family moving into a new house.
In real life, a local builder designs
an *actual* house for them to live in!

Raising six babies can be expensive—
help comes from everywhere!
A formula maker provides its
formula for free.

Swings and other supplies are
donated by manufacturers and
department store chains.

Even a twelve-seater van is loaned by a local car dealership. There's plenty of room for everybody—until you add six car seats, two grown-ups, formula, diapers, and several spare outfits.

Imagine how much time it takes just to get ready for a trip to the doctor!

All six babies are *fraternal*.
Each was born from a
separate egg.
None of the sextuplets are
exactly alike—not even a
pair are *identical*.

And, although the babies
share the same mom and
dad, they do *not* share the
same personality.

Brenna likes to
take care of
the others.
She's
Daddy's
little girl.

Julian's the clown, doing
pratfalls for fun and
roughhousing with his
brothers.

Quinn is the conscience of the group,
with a strong sense of right and wrong.

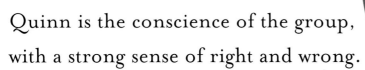

Claire is the ruler and role model, always the first to accomplish things.

Ian's the loner. He likes his own quiet time to make new discoveries.

And outgoing Adrian likes the thrill of adventure.

By the time they reach their *terrible twos*, the sextuplets are on the move.

Brenna and Claire are first on their feet, just two weeks ahead of the boys.

Like most multiples,
they started walking late,
but they are quick to make up
for lost time.

They play with everything,
touch everything, dump everything,
and learn to share.

14

By the time they are three,

there's a 3-tiered steel railing

in place of a playroom door

so no one can climb out

and make mischief.

Still it's fun to have six playmates—
all in the same family!

It's fun to have your own
secret language, too.
Just like many other multiples,
the sextuplets have their own
special language
no one else can understand.
Although they have normal intelligence,
learning to talk comes slowly.

At three, they say
single words
instead of sentences.
Mom and Dad use
puzzles and books to
speed up language
development.

Playtime can be
outside or inside,

all together,

alone, or with Mom or Dad.

The children eat lunch and dinner
on toddler-sized kitchen tables.
Then it's time for cleanup.
As part of their daily routine,
the tots help clear the tables
while Mom and Dad wipe
sticky faces.

Potty training is a routine, too—
though no one seems interested!

After dinner, it's bath time
with tub toys and splashing,
scrub-a-dub-dub,

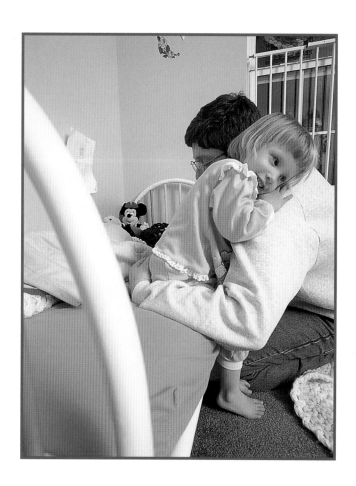

hugs and kisses,
and ready for bed.

"Goodnight, Brenna,

Quinn,

Julian,

Claire,

Ian,

and Adrian."

When it's time to rise and shine,
it's also time for school!

The sextuplets are the youngest
in their preschool class.
There's arts and crafts,
and lots of friends and fun.

Soon, six happy faces come home—
even the backpacks look pleased.

For their second
year of preschool,
Mom tries home-schooling.
Cutting colorful shapes is fun.

There are so many special times to remember . . .

babies' first Christmas,

a Valentine's Day of hearts and kisses,

a magical Halloween
with trick-or-treating,

and a very happy birthday.
Blow out four candles
and make six wishes!

This book is dedicated to Brenna, Julian, Quinn, Claire, Ian, and Adrian. We will always be thankful and inspired by the beautiful miracle of your lives.

The Dilleys would like to thank the following companies and individuals for their generosity in helping the family: Dr. David McLaughlin, Dr. Lynda Smirz, Dr. Betty Lou Walsman, Dr. Lydia Abab, Dr. Scott Curnow, Dr. Belinda Watts, all the nurses and the staff at Women's Hospital-Indianapolis, Cosco, Mead-Johnson, GM-Chevrolet, Gerber, and OshKosh B'Gosh.

Text copyright © 1998 by Becki and Keith Dilley
Photographs copyright © 1998 by E. Anthony Valainis

First published in the United States of America in 1998 by Walker Publishing Company, Inc.

Published simultaneously in Canada by Thomas Allen & Son Canada, Limited, Markham, Ontario.

Library of Congress Cataloging-in-Publication Data
Dilley, Becki.
Sixty fingers, sixty toes: see how the Dilley Sextuplets grow/Becki and Keith Dilley; photographs by E. Anthony Valainis.
p. cm.
ISBN 0-8027-8613-8 (hardcover). —ISBN 0-8027-8614-6 (reinforced)
1. Child rearing—United States. 2. Sextuplets—United States. 3. Child rearing—United States—Pictorial works. 4. Sextuplets—United States—Pictorial works. I. Dilley, Keith. II. Valainis, E. Anthony. III. Title.
HQ769.D462 1998
649'.144—DC21
97-23087   CIP

                    AC

Book design by Diane Stevenson and Janis Lotwin of Snap-Haus Graphics

Printed in Hong Kong

10 9 8 7 6 5 4 3 2 1